Colours and Numbers	page 2
1 Pets	page 4
2 School	page 18
3 Families	page 32
4 Body	page 44
Festivals: Christmas	page 58
Festivals: Easter	page 60
Words	page 62

Colours and Numbers

 Listen and point

OR

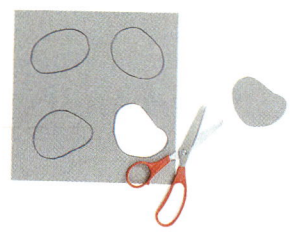

1 Find 4 stones.

1 Cut out 4 'stones'.

2 Write the words.

2 Write the words.

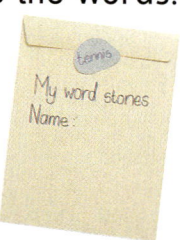

3 Keep the stones in the box.

3 Keep the 'stones' in the envelope.

 Sing

Colours

Red and yel low, blue and green,

blue and green, blue and green, red and yel low,

blue and green, black and white and brown.

 Say the rhyme

One Potato

One potato, two potatoes, three potatoes, four,
Five potatoes, six potatoes, seven potatoes, MORE!

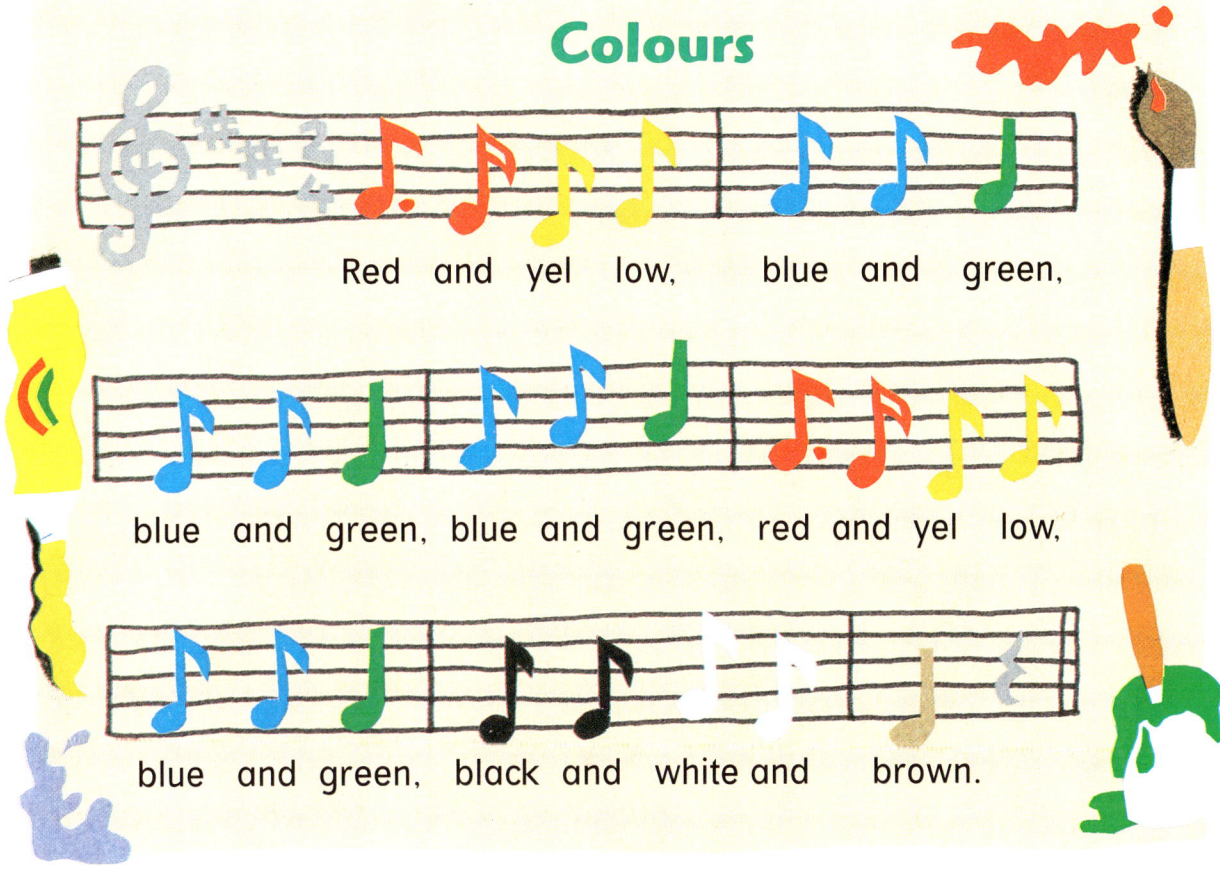

1 Pets

STORY

 **Kate's Snake**

Hi, Julie!

 Listen

Make

A Name Badge

You need

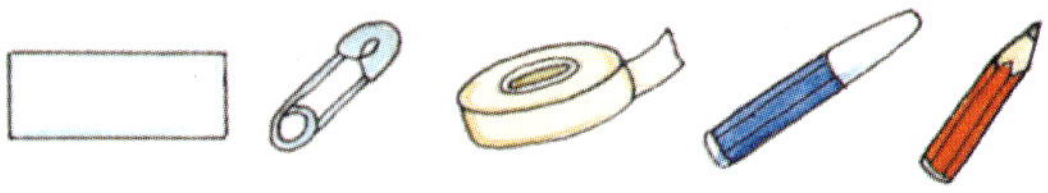

1 Write your name.

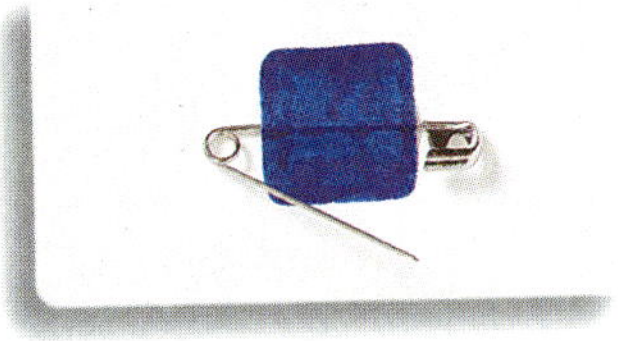

2 Stick the pin on.

3 A name badge.

Pets
1A

 **Ask and answer**

Who's this?   Julie.

Who's this?   Butch.

Who's this?   Kate.

Who's this?   Sam.

Who's this?   Kev.

Answer

Hello! I'm Kate. What's your name?

Hi! I'm Julie. What's your name?

7

Bill's Tortoise

 Listen

 Ask and answer

Pets
1B

 **Bingo Cards**

You need ▱ ▱ ▱ x 10

1 Write the names.   **2** Cover 4 pictures.   **3** Play.

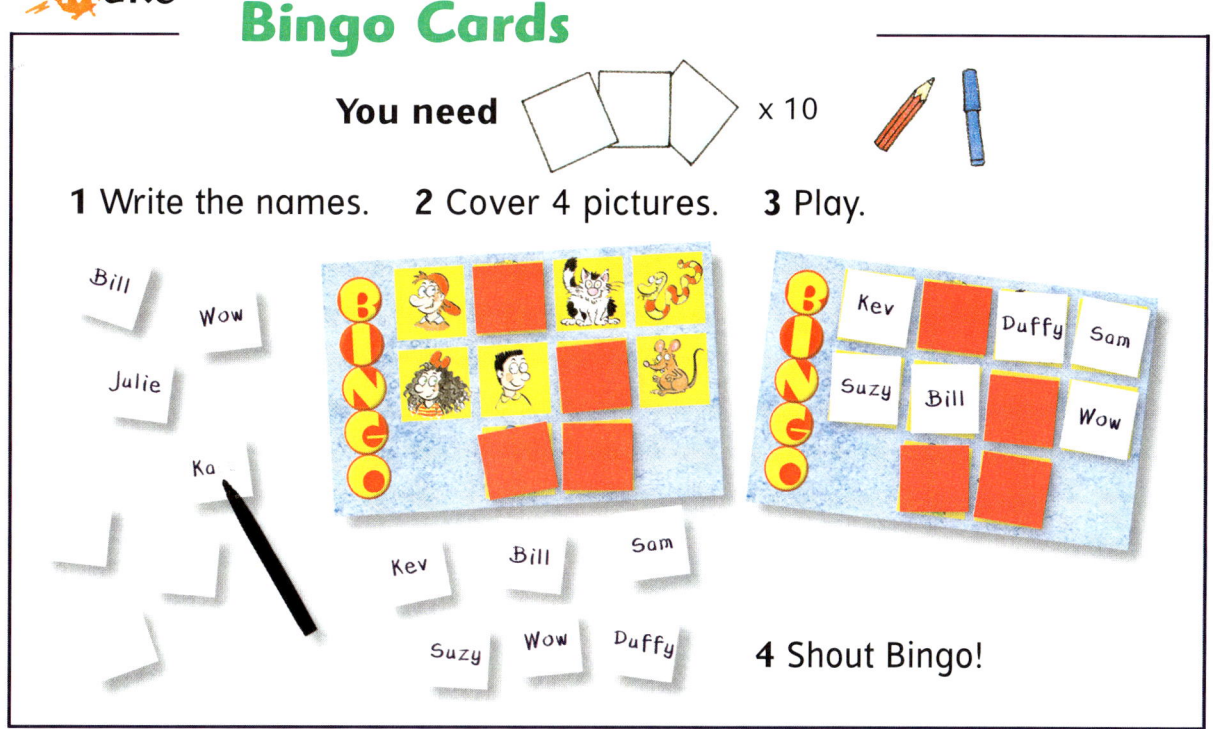

4 Shout Bingo!

9

Kev's Computer

 Listen

 Ask and answer

What's this?   What's this?   What's this?   What's this?   What's this?

A dog.   A cat.   A mouse.   A tortoise.   A snake.

Pets 1c

 Ask and answer

1 Is this Kev?

Yes.

2 Is this Sam?

No.

Ask and answer

Who's this?
What's this?
Is this ...?

Suzy's Drawings

 Listen

 Ask and answer

Is this a boy?

No, it's a girl.

Is this Kate?

No, it's Kev.

Is this a snake?

No, it's a tortoise.

Pets
1D

 Sing

Old MacDonald

Old MacDonald had a farm,
E-I-E-I-O
And on that farm he had a dog,
E-I-E-I-O
With a woof woof here and a woof woof there,
Here a woof, there a woof,
Everywhere a woof woof,
Old MacDonald had a farm,
E-I-E-I-O

 Ask and answer

What colour is Slow?	Green and brown.
What colour is Butch?	White.
What colour is Duffy?	Black and white.
What colour is Sam?	Red and yellow.
What colour is Wow?	Brown.

13

Words and Sentences

Use

Make

Pets

1E

 Find more words

- bird
- tortoise
- rat
- rabbit
- fish
- cat
- mouse
- snake
- dog
- hamster

15

START A PROJECT

Pets

1 F

SUPERSNAKE

- Hello, Wendy.
- Hello, Willy.
- Look! What's that?
- Is it a bird?
- Is it a plane?
- No! It's... Supersnake!

Make

A Snake

You need

1 Draw and colour.

2 Cut.

3 Stick.

4 Stick.

5 It's Supersnake!

17

2 School

STORY

 **Where's Wow?**

What's This?

 Listen

 Ask and answer

What's this?   A bag.

What's this?   A pencil.

What's this?   A book.

What's this?   A table.

What's this?   A chair.

School 2A

Sing

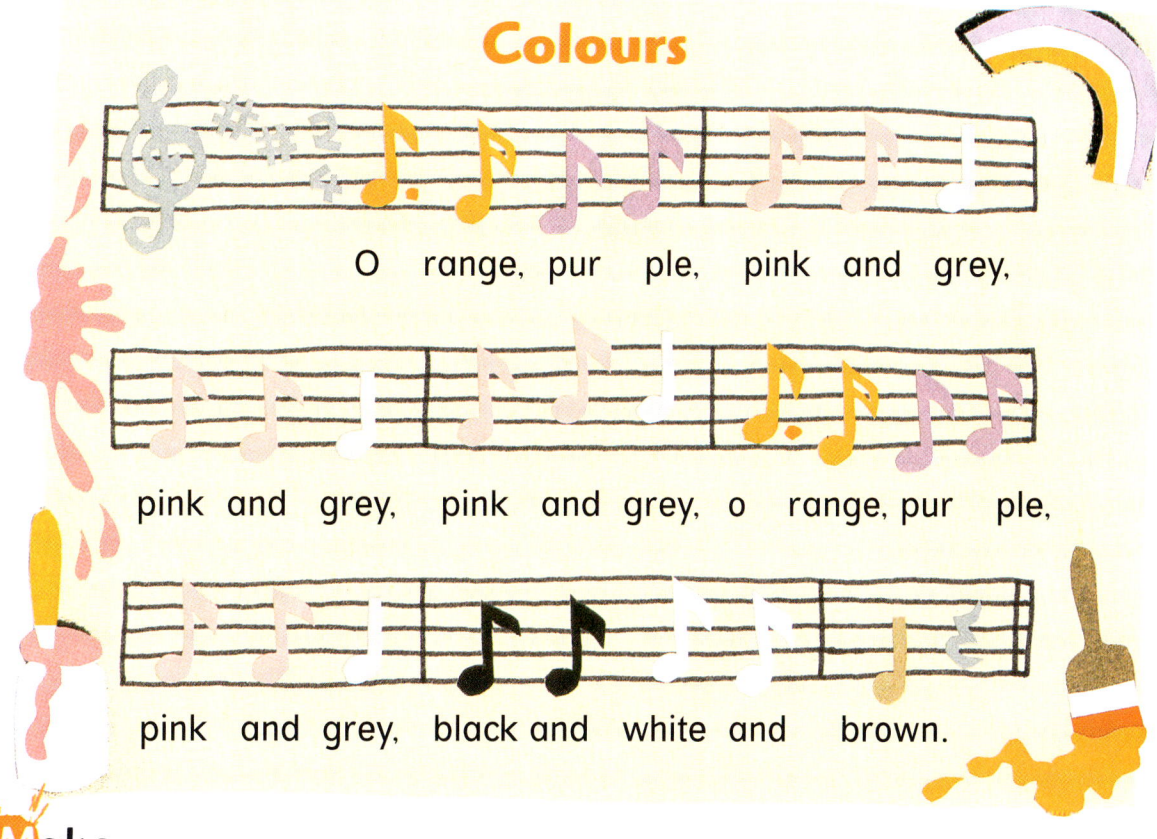

Make

A Spinning Top

You need

1 Colour the card red, blue, green and yellow.

2 Turn the card over.

3 Write the words bag, pencil, chair and book on the card.

4 Put a pencil through the card.

What Is It?

 **Listen**

 Ask and answer

   What's this?   A pen.

   What's this?   A rubber.

   What's this?   A ruler.

   What's this?   A pencil sharpener.

   What's this?   A pencil case.

School 2B

 Ask and answer

What's number 1?
I don't know.
Is it a door?
Oh, yes!

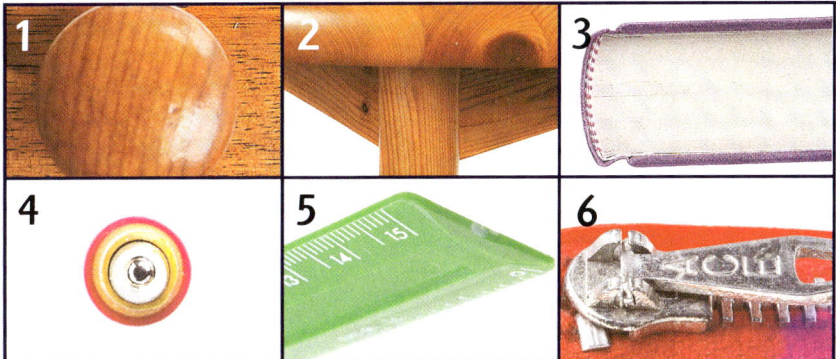

 Play

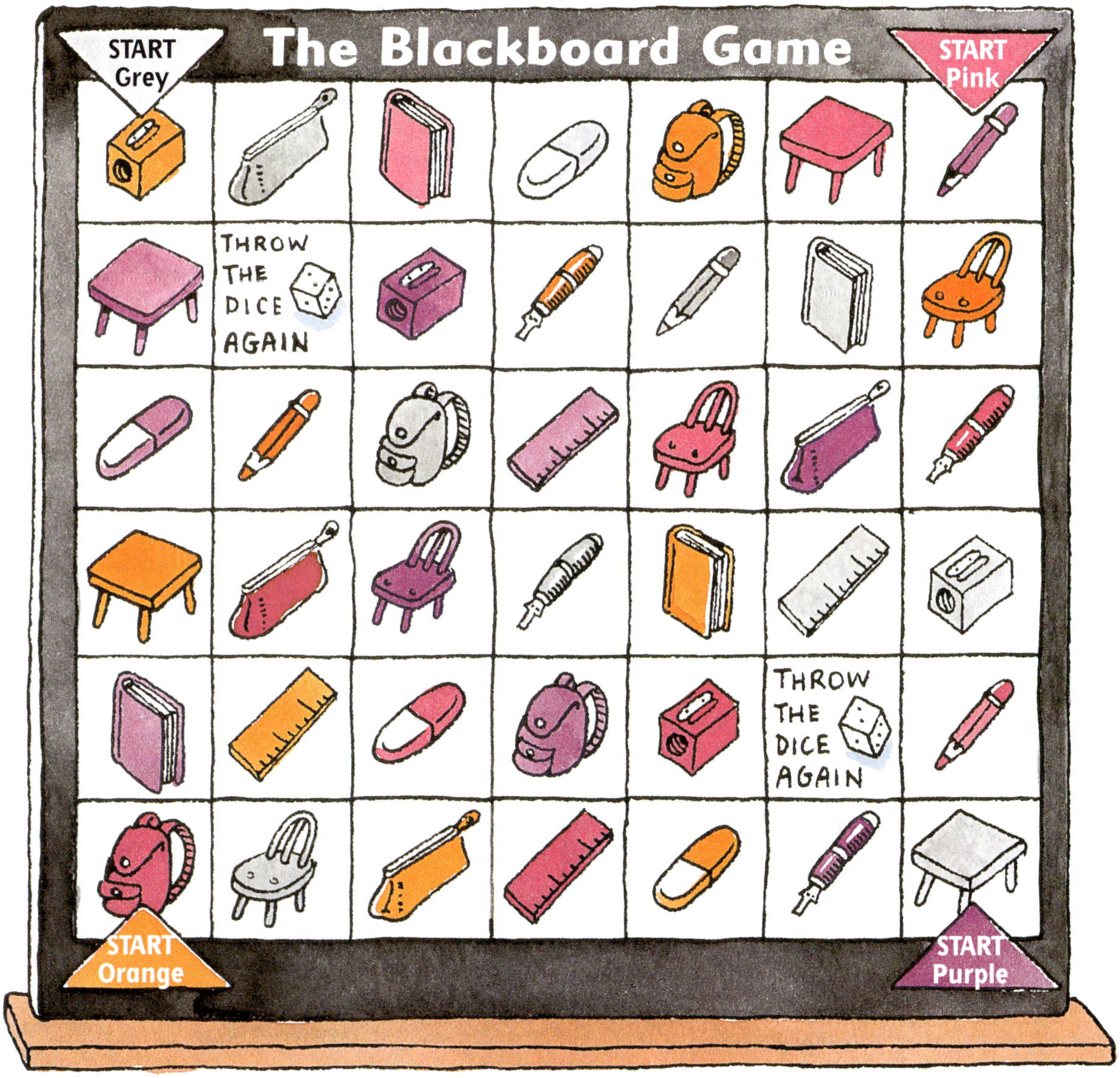

The Blackboard Game

How Many?

 Say the rhyme

One, two, three ...

One, two, three, four,
Please come in and shut the door.
Five, six, seven, eight,
It's time for school, you're very late.
Nine, ten, nine, ten,
Don't be late for school again!

School 2c

How many pencils?

one two three four

five six seven eight

nine ten

 ake **Number Flashcards**

You need ▢ ▢ ▢ x 20

1 Write the numbers.

2 Play games. Find the numbers.

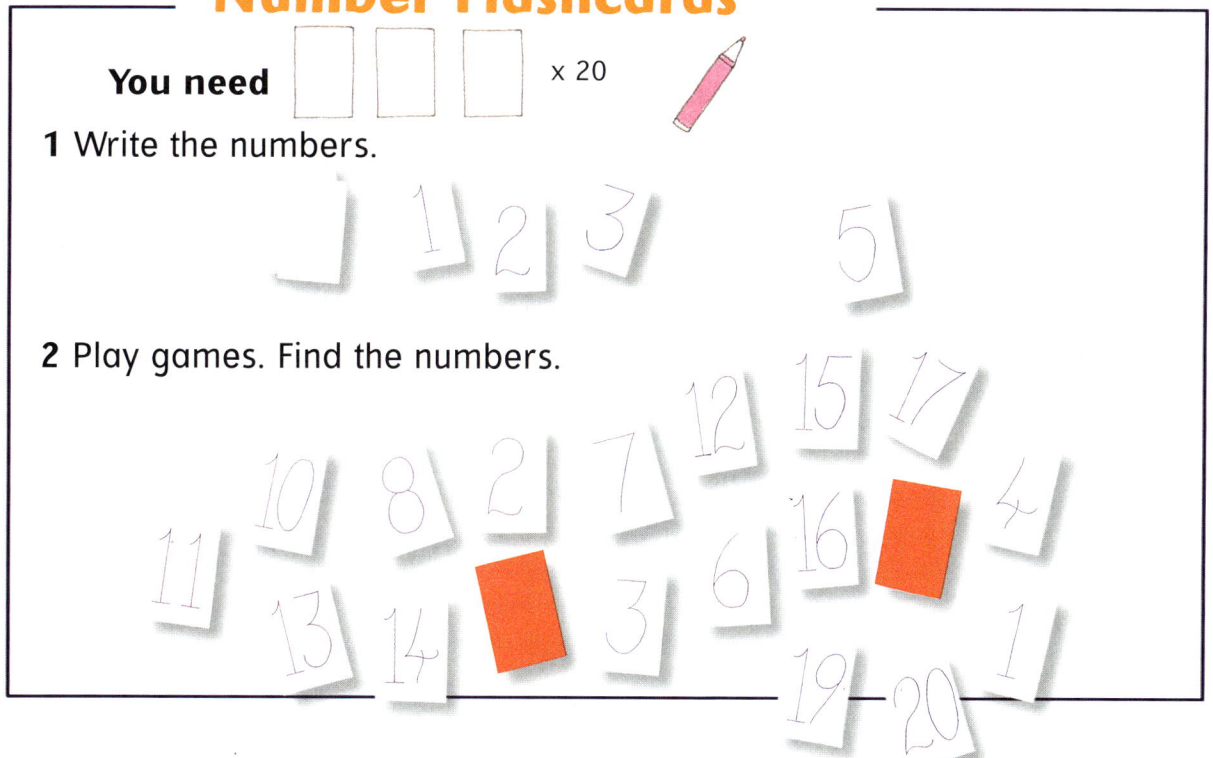

25

Where's the Rubber?

Play

Ask and answer

Where's the bag?	On the table.
Where's the pen?	In the box.
Where's the rubber?	Under the table.
Where's the ruler?	In the bag.

School 2D

🔊 Ask and answer

1   Where's the pencil?   It's in the bag.

🔊 Listen

27

Words and Sentences

Use

Make

28

School 2E

 Find more words

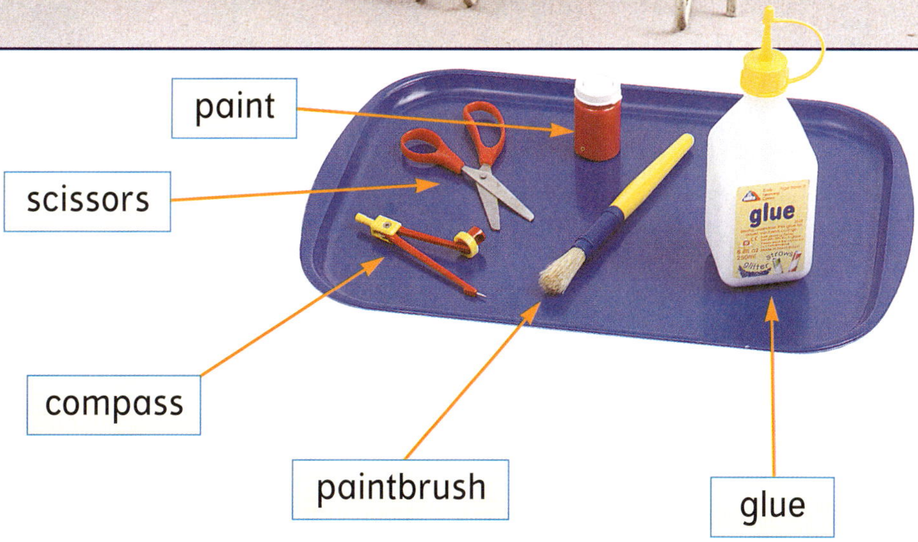

- clock
- computer
- cupboard
- desk
- bin
- paint
- scissors
- compass
- paintbrush
- glue

29

START A PROJECT

School
2F

3 Families

STORY

 **Family Photographs**

32

3

4

7

8

33

Who's That?

 Listen

 Listen

Families

3A

Ask and answer

Say the rhyme

How Many?

How many people live at your house?
One, my father,
Two, my mother,
Three, my sister,
Four, my brother.
There's one more. Now let me see.
Oh yes, of course. It must be me!

35

Happy Birthday

 Listen

 Sing

Happy Birthday to You!

Happy Birthday to you,
Happy Birthday to you,
Happy Birthday dear Gary,
Happy Birthday to you.

 Listen

36

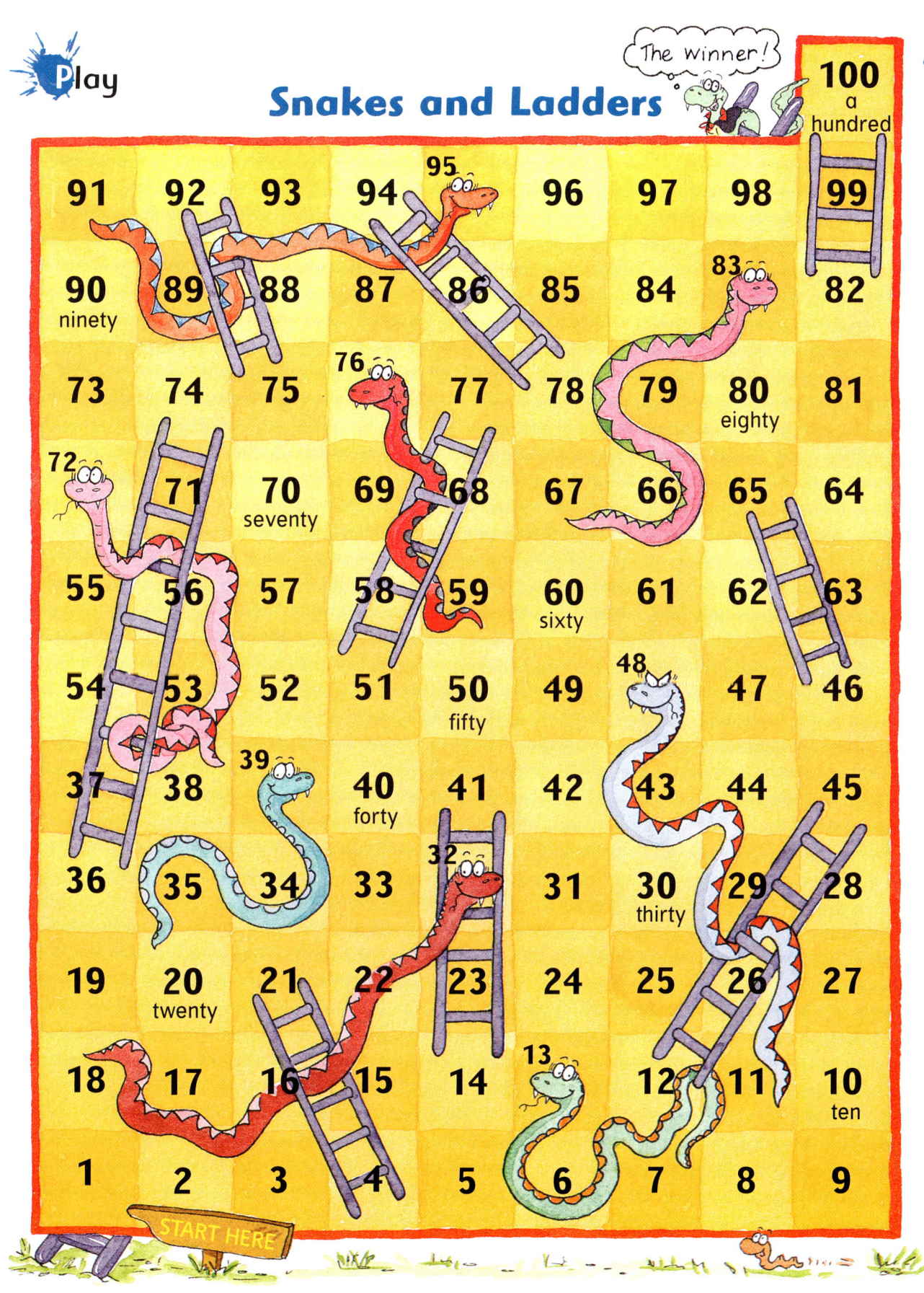

Play

Snakes and Ladders

The winner!

Families
3B

91	92	93	94	95	96	97	98	99	100 a hundred
90 ninety	89	88	87	86	85	84	83	82	
73	74	75	76	77	78	79	80 eighty	81	
72	71	70 seventy	69	68	67	66	65	64	
55	56	57	58	59	60 sixty	61	62	63	
54	53	52	51	50 fifty	49	48	47	46	
37	38	39	40 forty	41	42	43	44	45	
36	35	34	33	32	31	30 thirty	29	28	
19	20 twenty	21	22	23	24	25	26	27	
18	17	16	15	14	13	12	11	10 ten	
1	2	3	4	5	6	7	8	9	

START HERE

37

Bill's Friend

Listen

This is my friend, Kev.

Hello, Kev. How are you?

Fine, thanks.

Hi, Mum. Where's Duffy?

Here! She's on the table.

Oh, dear! Duffy isn't Wow's friend.

Ask and answer

Who's Kev?	Bill's friend.
Who's Gary?	Suzy's brother.
Who's Mr Kay?	Bill's father.
Who's Kate?	Kev's sister.
Who's Mr Mills?	Gary's grandfather.

38

Families

3c

🎧 **Listen and match**

🎧 **Listen**

I'm Bill Kay. I've got one brother and one sister. My sister's name is Suzy. She's eight years old. My brother's name is Gary. He's five years old.

I'm Suzy Kay. I've got two brothers. Their names are Bill and Gary. Bill is nine and Gary is five.

39

Words and Sentences

Word Stones

one two three four

Make

tree door

sun shoe

The Stepping Stones Game

Bill Kate's friend

Suzy Kev's sister

Kate Julie's

is

Kev

Bill's

Julie Suzy's brother

40

Families

3D

 Find more words

Happy Easter Aunt

WISHING YOU A HAPPY BIRTHDAY, DAD

Birthday Greetings, Uncle

Best Wishes on your Birthday, Cousin! 2 Today

Merry Christmas, Mum

Happy Mother's Day

To Grandad Happy Christmas

Happy Birthday Grandma

aunt   cousin   dad   grandad
grandma   mother   mum   uncle

41

START A PROJECT

Grandma
Name: Mrs Clark
Age: 62

Grandad
Name: Mr Clark
Age: 66

Grandma
Name: Mrs Evans
Age: 58

Grandad
Name: Mr Evans
Age: 59

Mum
Name: Mrs Evans
Age: 35

Dad
Name: Mr Evans
Age: 36

Sister
Name: Lucy
Age: 4

Me
Name: Tom
Age: 9

Brother
Name: Ben
Age: 6

Families

3E

SUPERSNAKE

- What's that?
- A card. It's Supersnake's birthday.
- How old is he?
- I don't know.
- Oh, dear! I haven't got a card for Supersnake.
- I've got an idea!

HAPPY BIRTHDAY

43

4 Body

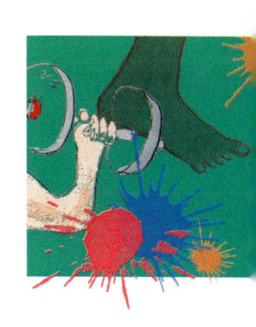

STORY

Hall of Mirrors

45

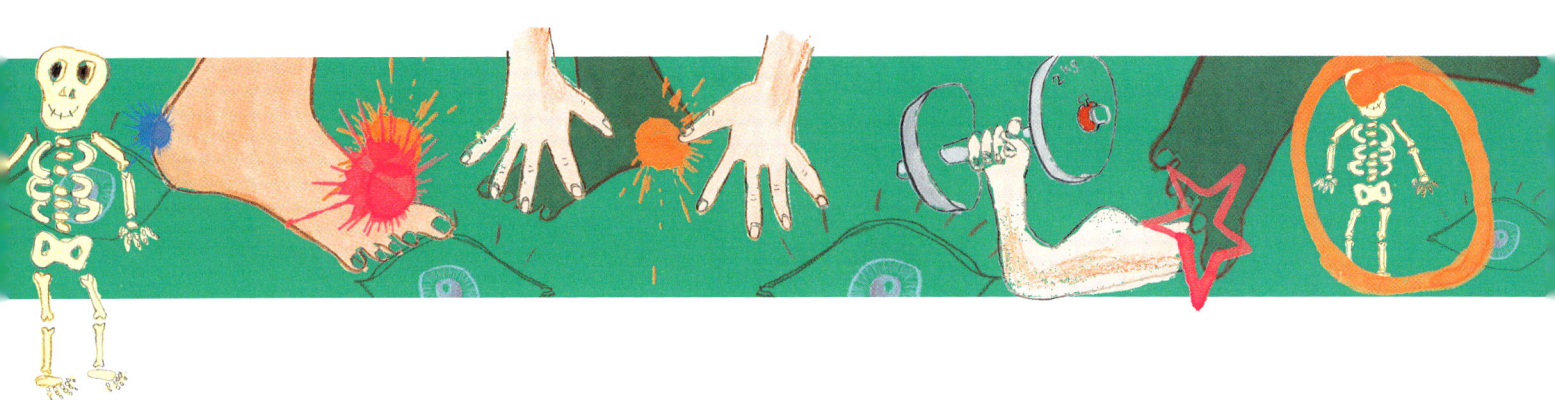

He's Tall and Thin

Listen

"Ha, ha! Look at Gary. He's tall and thin."

"Oooh! I'm small and fat and my hair is short."

Ask and answer

What colour is Julie's hair?   Blonde.

What colour are Julie's eyes? Green.

Body

4A

Ask and answer

How tall is Suzy?   1 metre 26 cm.

How tall is Kev?   1 metre 34 cm.

Ask and answer

Look at Julie in the mirror.

Is Julie small?   Yes.

Is Julie's hair long?   No, it's short.

Is Julie thin?   No, she's fat.

Faces and Monsters

Sing

Head and Shoulders ...

Head and shoulders, knees and toes,
Knees and toes.
Head and shoulders, knees and toes,
Knees and toes.
And eyes and ears and mouth
and nose.
Head and shoulders, knees and toes,
Knees and toes.

Make

A Face

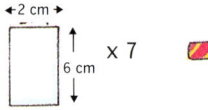

You need ▭ x 7

1 Draw the eyes: brown eyes, green eyes, blue eyes.

2 Draw two noses: one big nose, one small nose.

3 Draw two mouths: one big mouth, one small mouth.

4 Make a face.

48

Body
4B

Listen

This is the Monster family. Mother and father are called Zag and Zug. They've got three children, Zig, Zog, and little Zeg.

Ask and answer

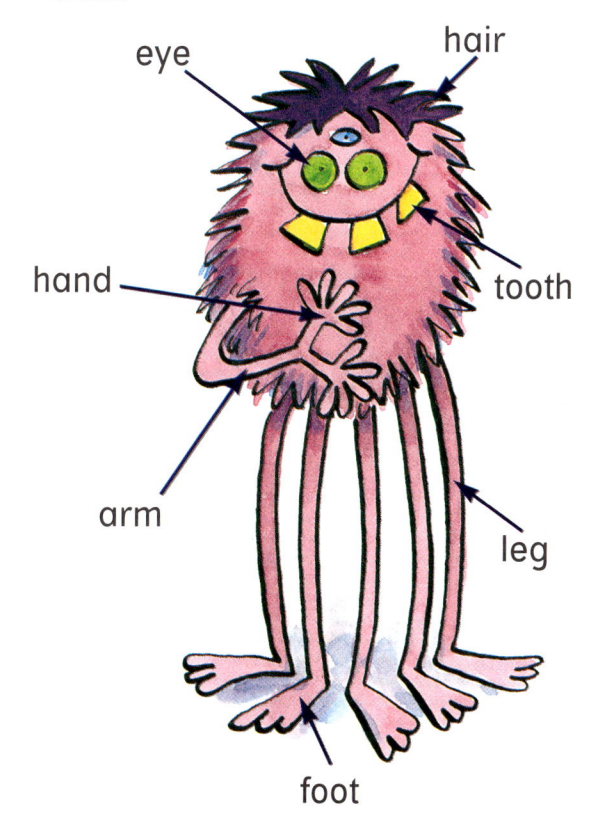

eye
hair
hand
tooth
arm
leg
foot

Zig is a big pink monster. His big eyes are green and his little eye is blue. His teeth are yellow. He's got two hands but only one arm. He's got five long legs and five feet. His hair is purple.

Is Zig small?	No, he's big.
How many eyes has Zig got?	Three.
How many legs has Zig got?	Five.
What colour is his hair?	Purple.

Two Big Ears

Play

THE MONSTER GAME — IF YOU DARE

KEEP OUT.

START HERE

1. Good start! Give your monster two big ears.
2. Friendly ghost. GO TO 4
3. Colour your monster green.
4. Give your monster black hair.
5. Draw a nose. Colour it blue.
6. Hairy spiders! GO TO 1
7. Give your monster a big nose.
8. Draw a big ear on your monster.
9. Draw four long arms.
10. Draw two big, blue eyes.
11. Draw four legs with big feet.
12. Bad cat! GO TO 10
13. Draw a big mouth and three long teeth.
14. Give your monster three fat legs.
15. Your monster's hair is short and pink.
16. Give your monster six red eyes.
17. Give your monster short arms and big hands.

Have you got a head and a body?

Give your monster a mouth and one tooth.

Go To 17

50

Body
4c

- Dracula! GO TO 22
- Give your monster two pink ears.
- 24 Draw three arms and three hands.
- 25 Draw a long nose.
- 26
- 27 Colour your monster purple.
- 28 Give your monster six arms.
- 23
- 22
- Colour it yellow.
- 21 Draw four little ears on your monster.
- 29 Draw six legs with small feet.
- 20 Draw two eyes. One big and one small.
- 30 Crocodile with big teeth! GO TO 26
- Angry rat! GO TO 15
- 19
- 31 Give your monster four orange eyes and three red eyes.
- 32 Give your monster a big, yellow nose.
- 33 Give your monster long, blonde hair.
- 34 Draw a mouth with four big teeth.
- 35 Give your monster one leg, one foot and three big toes.
- 36 Draw purple hair on your monster.
- 37 Finished? Yes - GO UP No. GO DOWN TO 17
- Go To 17
- THE END
- DANGER
- Go To 17

51

One Finger, One Thumb ...

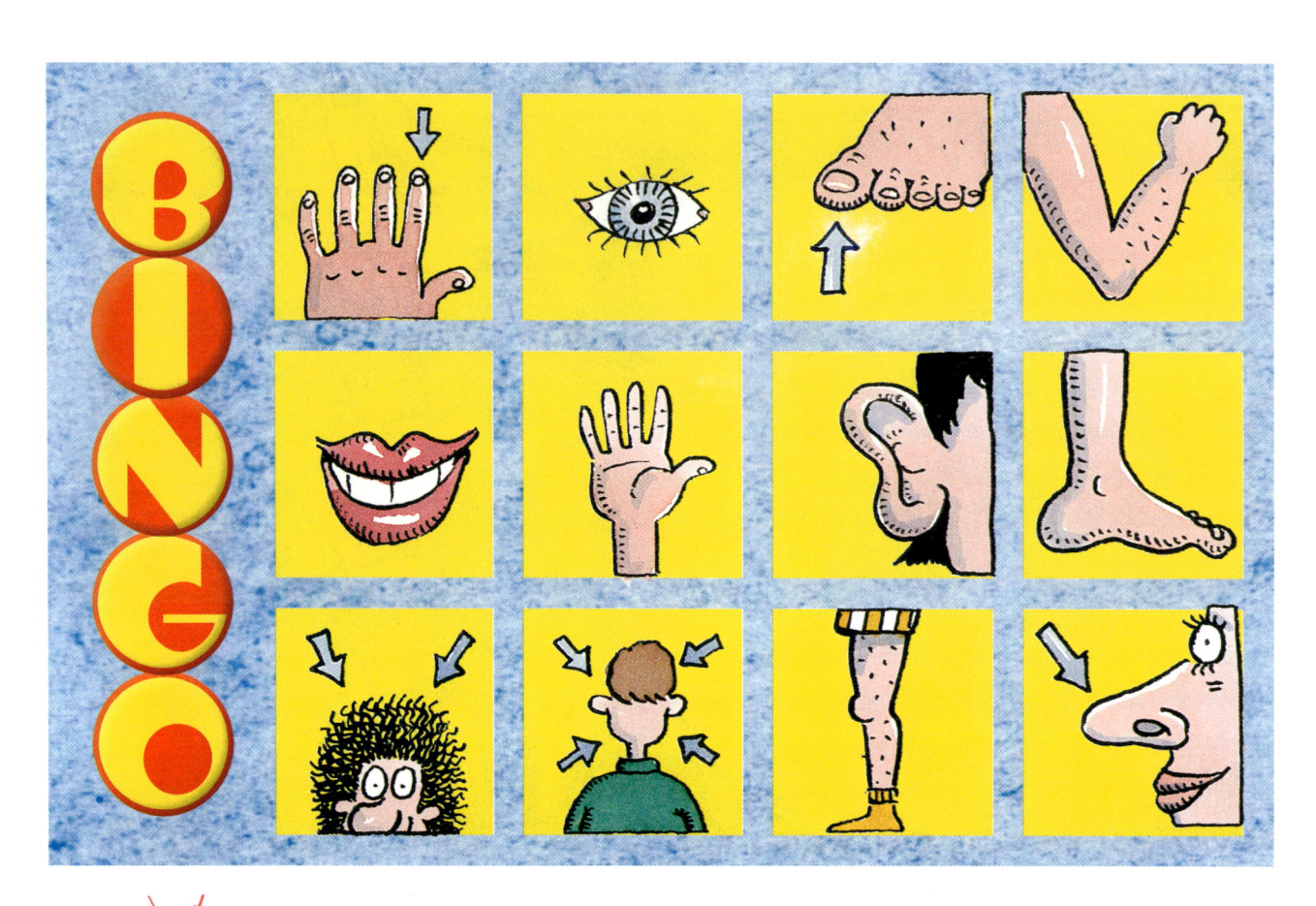

One Finger, One Thumb ...

One finger, one thumb, keep moving.
One finger, one thumb, keep moving.
One finger, one thumb, keep moving.
We'll all be happy today.

One finger, one thumb,
One arm, one leg, keep moving ...

One finger, one thumb, one arm, one leg,
One nod of the head, keep moving ...

One finger, one thumb, one arm, one leg,
One nod of the head,
Stand up, sit down, keep moving ...

Body
4D

Play

Queenie

Queenie

Queenie, Queenie,
Who's got the ball?
Is she big or is she small?
Is she fat or is she thin?
Or is she like a rolling pin?

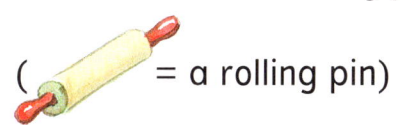

(= a rolling pin)

Listen

My Monster
by Kev Brown

This is my monster.
It's called Bulldog.
It's green, purple, red and blue.
It has got thirty eyes. It has
got three mouths. It has got
four long legs and five long
arms. It has got three noses.

Words and Sentences

Word Stones

Use

football, house, cake, taxi, tree, sun, hotel, glue, frog, sink, tennis, kite, hat, door, shoe, bed

The Stepping Stones Game

He, She, has, got, long, short, big, small, black, grey, blonde, brown, blue, green, hair, eyes

Body
4E

Find more words

teeth

lips

glasses

nose and moustache

beard and moustache

55

START A PROJECT

56

Body 4F

SUPERSNAKE

- Hello, Little Red Worm. What's that?
- A basket for my grandmother.
- Let's go! Quickly!
- Over there. There's my grandma's house.
- Aha! A rat. Wait here, Little Red Worm.
- Hello, Grandma.
- What a big nose you've got!
- What big teeth you've got!
- You're not a worm. You're a rat!
- And I'm not a worm.
- Aagh! It's Supersnake!
- Thank you, Supersnake.

57

Festivals

CHRISTMAS

We Wish You a Merry Christmas

We wish you a Merry Christmas,
We wish you a Merry Christmas,
We wish you a Merry Christmas,
And a Happy New Year!
Glad tidings we bring,
To you and your kin.
We wish you a Merry Christmas,
And a Happy New Year!

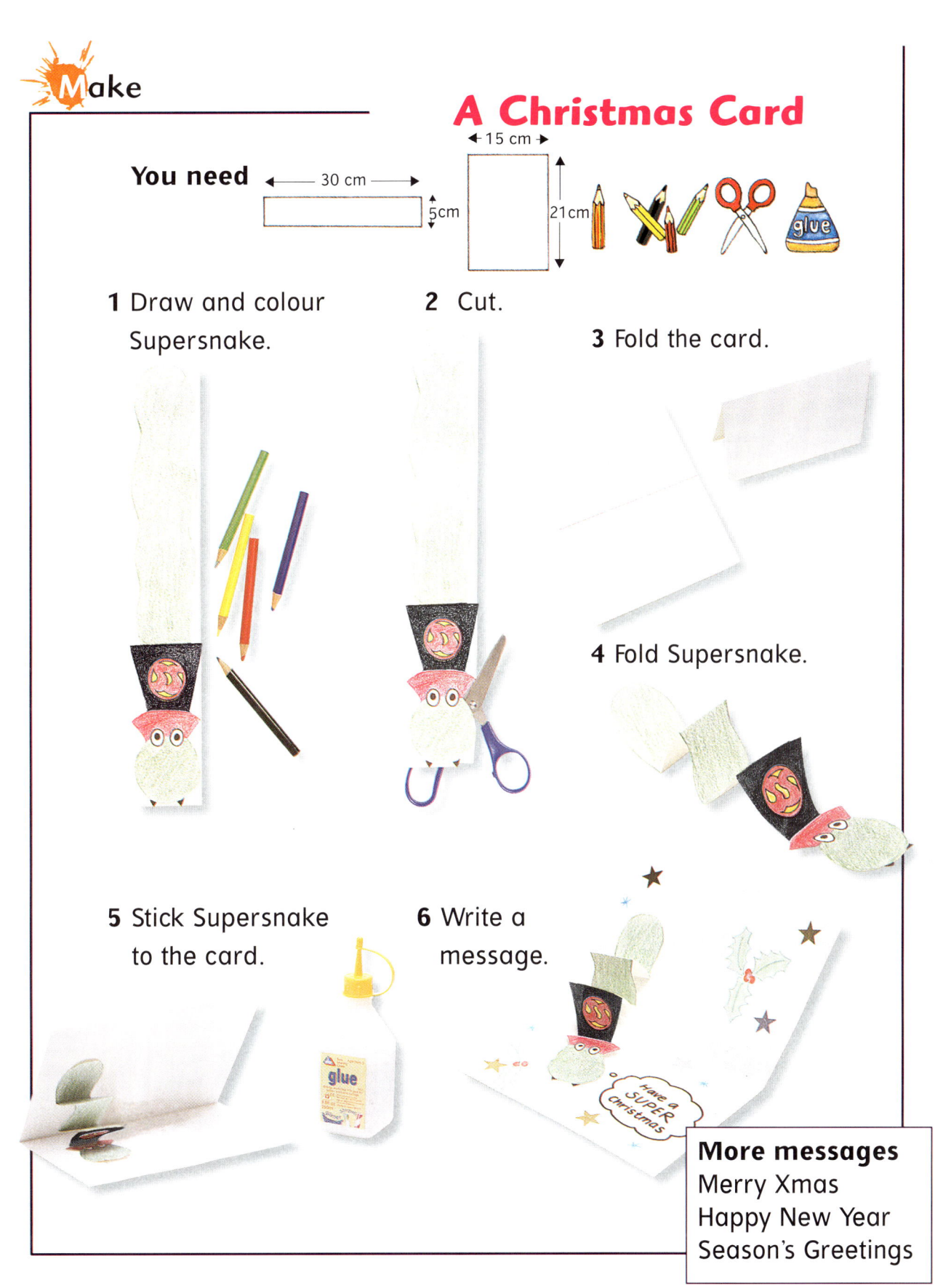

Make

A Christmas Card

You need ← 30 cm → ← 15 cm → 5cm 21cm

1 Draw and colour Supersnake.

2 Cut.

3 Fold the card.

4 Fold Supersnake.

5 Stick Supersnake to the card.

6 Write a message.

More messages
Merry Xmas
Happy New Year
Season's Greetings

59

Festivals

EASTER

Play

Egg Rolling

Find a hill. Everybody has a painted egg. Roll the eggs down the hill. The last egg to break is the winner!

Look and find

How many eggs are there?

Make

A Painted Egg

You need

1 Boil an egg for 5 minutes.

Ask an adult to help!

2 Put the egg in cold water for 10 minutes.

3 Paint a face or a pattern on the egg.

Words

Colours
black
blue
brown
green
grey
orange
pink
purple
red
white
yellow

Numbers
one
two
three
four
five
six
seven
eight
nine
ten
eleven
twelve
thirteen
fourteen
fifteen
sixteen
seventeen
eighteen
nineteen
twenty
thirty
forty
fifty
sixty
seventy
eighty
ninety
a hundred

Pets
bird
cat
dog
fish
frog
hamster
mouse
rabbit
rat
snake
tortoise

School
bag
bin
blackboard
book
box
chair
classroom
clock
compass
computer
cupboard
desk
dice
door
glue
moustache
mouth
nose
shoulder
thumb
toe
tooth (teeth)
paint
paintbrush
pen
pencil
pencil case
pencil sharpener
rubber
ruler
scissors
table
teacher

People
aunt
boy
brother
children
cousin
dad
family
father
friend
girl
grandad
grandfather
grandma
mum

Words

Mrs
sister
uncle

Body
arm
beard
ear
eye
face
finger
foot (feet)
hair
hand
head
knee
leg
lips

Adjectives
angry
bad
big
blonde
fat
friendly
hairy
happy
long
short
small
tall
thin

Prepositions
in
on
under

Questions
How?
How many?
What?
Where?
Who?

Greetings
Happy Birthday
Happy Easter
Happy New Year
Hello (Hi!)
How are you?
Fine, thanks.
Goodbye (Bye!)
Merry Christmas
Season's Greetings

Expressions
Come here!
I don't know
I've got an idea
Let's go!
Look!
Of course
Oh, dear!
OK
Please
Right
Thank you (Thanks)
Wrong

Classroom Language
Ask and answer
Close
Colour
Cover
Cut
Don't...
Draw
Give
Guess
Listen
Make
Match
Open
Pick up
Play
Point to
Put down
Read
Repeat
Say the rhyme
Shout
Sing
Sit down
Stand up
Start a project
Stick
Stop
Touch
Turn around
Walk
Write